LISTENING

BOOKS BY MARGARET AVISON

Winter Sun (1960)

The Dumbfounding (1966)

sunblue (1978)

Winter Sun/The Dumbfounding:
Poems 1940–66 (1982)

No Time (1989)

Selected Poems (1991)

A Kind of Perseverance (1994)

Not Yet But Still (1997)

Concrete and Wild Carrot (2002)

Always Now: The Collected Poems
(3 volumes, 2003–2005)

Momentary Dark (2006)

Listening: Last Poems (2009)

LISTENING

last poems

MARGARET AVISON

McCLELLAND & STEWART

LIBRARY AND ARCHIVES CANADA CATALOGUING IN PUBLICATION

Avison, Margaret, 1918-2007
Listening : the last poems / Margaret Avison.

ISBN 978-0-7710-0886-3

I. Title.

PS8501.V5L58 2009   C811.'54   C2008-904232-8

We acknowledge the financial support of the Government of Canada
through the Book Publishing Industry Development Program and
that of the Government of Ontario through the Ontario Media
Development Corporation's Ontario Book Initiative. We further
acknowledge the support of the Canada Council for the Arts and the
Ontario Arts Council for our publishing program.

Typeset in Aldus by M&S, Toronto
Printed and bound in Canada

This book is printed on acid-free paper that is 100% recycled,
ancient-forest friendly (100% post-consumer recycled).

McClelland & Stewart Ltd.
75 Sherbourne Street
Toronto, Ontario
M5A 2P9
www.mcclelland.com

1 2 3 4 5   13 12 11 10 09

CONTENTS

LISTENING

My aunts are robust. I
still have all
four. Do
yours come vividly
to mind at mention of
a comment at first
glimpse of the
no longer new baby?

"*Look* at the X nose
on the wee face!" (or
any kinship-logo-feature they
spot, or think they do).

That may be why
the X family keeps
a keepsake portrait of great-
grandfather Jock in the
dark on
the front stairs landing but
not near enough for you
to stand and view it.

THE RITE BECOME RIGHT

One particular name is
given. It
means, promises to
live under heaven till the full-
grown becomes bodily and
implicitly all
that meaning's
scent and spectrum and
echoes of progenitors', perhaps; its
tonal range and theme,
development, rising and falling
cadences until
the coda: utterance
fulfilled.

All that's in a name.

Choose carefully enough to
approach the precious
Gift-giver and
receive, to give.

LISTENING (FOR GRANDMA)

Our language You
speak! "They
are
His words," a kindly
elder assured her
granddaughter, as though
unwilling to put something on
me, not able not to.

The "words" she singled
out, I
listened to; they had
for me no heft.

Words up in the
air they'd seemed, blown eastward with
the early spring winds. When I am old
perhaps I will be savouring the
squirrelling words at play in
my innermost branches?

Once, for good, came the discovery.
Print privately can be-
come Voice, speaking
words the lost
grandmother
kept long ago, in-
structing me, hoping

some murmur down the years,
some lilt of holy love
would linger till I too
knew. Those
words, still hers, now
murmur within, massy as a
golden heirloom,

astonish me with how
real words are. Oh
yes, I can skid
over surfaces and
syllables. But "real
words" are the
ones Your mouth-parts, throat
and breath
weigh in with, meanings
soundlessly deep forever.

TWO WHOMS *or* I'M IN TWO MINDS

Whenever I say, or even think:
all, launching out upon a
train of thought, then
such a clamour –
                    we're coming, we're about
ready, don't go without . . .

Without – whom?

The barley-broom in long grass
(hushed in its silken plumage),
one or two beads picked off my
childhood's dear fringed lampshade
still bright, perhaps a
vintage elm – that last
evening, in good old summertime
before the move out West (recalled
regularly by my
resolute father athirst for clear brook
water babbling over stones all deep
in blanketing snow).

How many are there
of you? Would it strike you as
better if I'd said,
"Whenever I think, or say,
everything . . ."?

Thing! What do *you* think?

All right then, that's
out, and the end
of *all* as well.
Now permit me to insist on
elaborating the thoughts I was
headed for . . .

You plan to do
that in
words?

      To
whom do I defer, now?

Words. Fancy,
for instance, saying that
Aplectrum hyemale (one of the
orchids) is the same as
Putty Root (its other name)!

Well, it *is* the
same plant.
Might we not both acknowledge
the borders? My
territory, the realm of truths, their
history, their
implications, and the
outworking in our ways.
                And yours

the fields of, what?
Particles?

I like the word
"particulate." Its dictionary
meaning has slipped my mind. But
do let's have a cluster of
particulates that I can
dance among, with castanets.

Peace be between and to
us, both!

FOR THE CHILDREN'S QUESTIONS

What is this glinting
deep (or gasping uprush);
the "why, how, when" of it? To
know a
focus be-
speaking the
depthless, all-high au-
thority, there is a
quick reply: "Melchi-
zedek!"* No more
until not one is
left any
longer with
a "when."

<hr>

* "Melchizedek": Psalm 110:4
Hebrews 7

ARCHITECTURE

The white and gold of a
cold morning, with
March through the door to-
morrow's daybreak, sets
the pulses throbbing. Oh
I know the heaviest snow-
falls have been March's. Nine-
teen thirty-six saw single-file
foot traffic down
Yonge Street. Many who went,
set out to go, to
work, walked all they could,
wading thigh-deep at times
until, in any
coffee-shop or pub
someone had managed to open by then,
they met and talked with
whatever other venturer
chose to be stranded there.

Within pedestrian per-
imeters, the normally pre-
occupied metropolis
discovers itself, here,
as a small community on a
snowy morning, whitely
distinct.

Let the snow fly. The winds
heap it into its smooth
sheets for drafting-boards. Let
anyone bring a vision, not of
glimmering ice, but of
ivory palaces, rising
this day.

And let who will climb on
the stool there, seize the pencil in
silence to
measure out his
initial line.

A LINGERING TOUCH

Last year's pussy willows
branch about all
winter in
a dry pewter vase.
Their corner table is
back by the
drapes where
the east
windows begin.

Yesterday, after
winter, March's sun
felt warm on the skin.
This morning as he
mounted towards zenith, one
shone-in shaft
played, puss by puss
slowly, up
the southmost stalk of the
pussy willows.
Why, its playing was
music,
a slow progression towards
the final
treble salute.

RELEASES

Gold is the sun among
little new leaves. The
prisoner, on his wife's
arm, on his daughter's
other arm, wonderingly
blinks into the
new day; he is released.

Evidence is sifted in
box-rooms windowless often. The
condemned is fleetingly
outdoors again. Even being
bundled into their car, he breathed
sun and tarpots. He was
safer for the fort-
ification of the one
sky over all his thirty-eight
years of daytime.

In the cell too there was
a glimpse of sky: sometimes at "exercise" a
rain-dark smell like a
stripped birch's his hand had once
cupped, soapy and smooth, with a
tang even in the touch.

Famished for all the
velvety greens and skittering squirrels, the

incarcerated – no wonder! – some
days lay, blaming
the pointlessness of penned-in
people, blaming the
one outside who wouldn't
step forward, make amends. Until
he did, no uniformed officer would
face it: they'd
caged the wrong bird.
Motivation would have to be
stronger than that!

When Pilate delivered Jesus over to
the guard, Jesus was blameless
and Pilate knew it.
Has any son or
daughter of a woman ever
since been blameless?
Truth will out, in life or
afterwards, a commit-
ment, maybe a growing, one-
day towering
menace?

He stepped forward! Why? Because his
skies, ever since, had
seemed to deny him the
freedom to swing along, walking as if
weightless, delivered over
to the incurious, all-
seeing sky.

Release, originally, meant
"to leave behind," a being left
behind!

A good American dict-
ionary gives the current
meaning (for him, and his
relaxing family): "let go,
set free."

Back where the icejam
breaks, where frolicking waters
foam and swirl down, up, over, flooding
wintry fields and rutted roads, the scramble for
deliverance is, this day,
in all its senses widely,
widely understood.

STILL LIFE

The last two daffodils
are dying on my table.
What were once petals grope
for water, can no longer
sip, though they stand in water,
must grope the air for more.
They have transmuted from
flower to scrawny
fingers, an old woman's in
raggedy silk gloves.

The only future for
a dying flower is
compost-mash: its lingering
memorial, when the first
eggshell dawn
lifts up a new
horizon, all
in stemless daffodils,
flowering.

SLOW START

Thankfulness overflows from the
gold rim and royal purple of this
rainy day's
low dawning. On the
muddle of not yet un-
differentiated clouds
stray
marbling streaks.

None of it could be
eyed head-on, no
scald for
nakedly receiving
day, almost before it's
launched. (Anticipatory,
that watery verb?)

FORETASTE, CANADIAN

I have seen the valley trees
receive Your
bud-breaking, slowly savour
golden-green life in
late April's balmy
foreglimpse of
summertime's benefice:
shadows' touch, for little
us "like trees walking"* to
receive as do the trees in
lavish springtime's
early first-green im-
pulse.

---

* "like trees walking": Mark 8:24

OCULAR

Glimpse of a driveway, in the flush
of Mayday joy, deceived:
I saw it as a lilac bush
among the dancing leaves.

Often the not-so-distant scene
becomes, to aged eyes,
a somehow valid might-have-been
discerned with glad surprise.

MISCONSTRUING

Don't we tend to
twist lines, try to ad lib some
"general sense" of
what the words mean?
A new dictionary
we can devise?

The word "abominable," for instance,
makes sense only if *all*
human beings are
"testified against" – the root is
omen.

Maybe that makes good sense.

Sixteenth-century trans-
lators were more skilful
in reading lines
acceptably. They *invented* a
root *ab-hominem*; perhaps
evoking a father's moment of
scalding discouragement:
"Go to your room! Think
about your abominable
behaviour – after all
we've done for you!"

Or, perhaps, they were
groping for
the opposite of "loveable."

The misreading evokes a
thickening gentleman who
knew the tailor's
larger waist was a good
fit, but hankered
to try a smaller . . .

                    He was
misreading "fit" because
he didn't want to face its
meaning, yet.

White in the night the
eyeballs shine. They are
anchored by strings
that radiate out from a
point in-
side that head, but within
a delicate petal-work of
lashes and lids.
               Are these rolled back
in the dark to
stare at the sourceless
light mirrored deep in the night
in eyeball-shine?

O tell the invisible
vigil-keeper: it's
moonlight surely,
even in the
dark of the moon.

                        presses in
upon a person to that moment sure he is
mature now, coping, in
balance: with
tree-shadow on his watered flower-
borders (or, trees to sketch
their etchings on his snowdrifts).

Eyes from behind the Cloud
see him, see through. It is
oddly bracing, that pressure. Being
seen, surprisingly
opens his eyes to a
feather, white and indigo, on
a granular leaf his
rake had not prodded away.

The Cloud embraces his
opened eyes, himself as
well. Lost,
he is without
focus awhile. A name from
years back warbles its
alerting secret: Richard
Rolle of Hampole.

The Cloud, too strange to
see, now, fingers,

takes careful prongs, unsettles
all that was fixed,
opens out the
wild beyond his
glossy hedges.

Out of the Cloud
(within now)
fingers, or delicate prongs,
pick out, shift, a
morsel here, a
crumb of his old
person, there.
                   He no longer
feels bulged in
on, as at first.
Let the years
ahead (perhaps)
tune him up, his
listening ear, tune even
perhaps his knowing that
now, he can
play in.

Suddenly the One,
given, constant, good,
entered. If we try to
welcome Him as a
treasure-bearer, "Thank you!,"
He turns, head down. A
celebratory instant be-
comes a noiseless
poignancy, redolent,
enveloping but, abruptly,
circumscribed.

Thanking an evening star for
meeting your eye is different. Distance
is not rebuke. That ancient
light, received, keeps no count of
mothers' children's children's chil-
dren (ultimately us, un-
til we too in
turn pass
on the heritage).

At full or at
ebbing tide, the welcomed One
has His own in and
outflowing purposes.
Already we are bonded. None-
theless the eternal

Person is
willing to
watch with me, listen, look
ahead, knowing
His host must joyfully in
time
yield to some not
yet visible to me
design.

A creator of all that is
to be perfect would be
,yes, all-knowing. But
that would be an
imperfection without
the spice of now and then
wincings, and . . .
wit? Rather, a
lingering
in a dark
ingle, in mischievous
midsummer. There in secret can
be devised
risky assemblages of
as-if-unpredictables?
                       Was
that where we
came in?

And since the perfect is
self-consistent, did it in-
volve more daring:
tentatively, to un-
tether the rash
rover – a prank
just for the wink of an
eye's instant?

26

When it turns out that we,
made, find it
oddly fun occasionally, in
spite of
that and this (everyone's
itemizables)?

When is it best? When the
Maker, betimes, can
relax aside, com-
posing His own di-
vertimentos! Then, oh then, let
anticipation stir. Let there
be sometime galas –
out of the blue. "You are
invited. R.S.V.P."

METAMORPHOSIS

Why are we so
often not
any different? Oh there are
changes nobody tried to
make happen but on a
workaday level, never from
silence's special
place where it's as if
periwinkle faces play at
being zenith:
                        up, up so
mirror-silent the
glassy dimness shows the
one far flower, here, or
almost blindingly
aloft, as well.

PILGRIM

As the Creator made
every orb and places
where they could roll, and every
ocean, each with its beaches and
promontories so there could be
land greening day by day,
at peace in the dark hours, He
saw that it was good.

                          Oh why
make man to make of them and of
ourselves, a desert?
Has He prepared in
our spoiled world an avenue for
His coming?

Many say "Nonsense!" Even some
ecologists, although
intent on rueing and
restoring, are
shaken about human good intentions.

A few are
wistful, elegiac
for what, once, was
loveliness.

It takes a breath-catching
simplicity, a
belief in a
purposive, no matter if
any-which-way ongoing, plus
intervals. (Why
that oompah-oompah merry-go-round the
dizzied parent divines in its
sulphurous shiny yellows etc? Some
impulse of new energy
may have evoked that
irrelevant fantasy.)
                      This is
now, to do: plough through
up-ended chunks of paving, litter,
wrecked window-casings, then
scuff through the dust and
bristles of a
(once) farm.
                    That's hard.

The pilgrim flounders on,
aware of them? of Him? away
beyond the
thunderous silence of
the universe.
                      Nevertheless, it's hard to
              trust, now, in a trail, still up
              ahead opening. Will there
              be basswood leafing out? Or will there even be

a dead-end at a
vast curtain?
            The Hand may draw it back, no
mechanism involved, on all
the rolling spheres, even
that outermost, all-embracing
orb: foreverness.

FLAMING?

Rip-roaring fire is possible but
panic-proof never; the frantic
rescuer is
lost when fear-
frozen. Fire, we
respect, even when we
have made it, built up
the kindling, snapped
lengths off the branches to add,
and lit,
let it all
catch, set drafts and fire-
screen, readied the log, and
whisked the hearth clean of flammable
bits.

How can it be that
"consuming fire"* awaits us
warmly, so that a few who
had frozen with terror, come
to in time to be
made comfortable in the near
warmth as well?

_____

* "consuming fire": Deuteronomy 4:24
                              Hebrews 12:29

And who are these who seem
impervious to peril, these
adventurers, explorers,
routinely on the rim of the unknown,
heedless about
finding a way back home?
Fire licks
at anything dry. No matter!
Reason's first and
last resort, deliberate
reconsideration, is an an-
aesthetic under danger, even
transmittable, even to a few
withering generations.

                        Flames
entice high-stepping fellows
barely out of their teens. They
leap towards the holy
fire in an
all-alone world where one
glimpse would wind them in
as well: wonderfully
unscorched although aglow!

HEAVEN

O God in heaven Your home, where
were You when You built it into
breath-catching beauty? Or is
heaven perhaps
simple? A bare
throne-room, unadorned?

You endure
spareness, perhaps, enduring
down through the eons, in
the knowledge that beyond
dreary emptiness lies
a Day.

On that day, ready at
last, prepared by
Your blueprint, all
Your servants: archi-
tects, dry-wall men, brick-
layers (or stone-
masons) and gem-
cutters, each one's
developed art or craft
wholeheartedly
realizing Your so long
unworked, perfect design!

It's true, isn't it? You
were willing to
wait because
it will be Your day too, with
crowding-in courtiers glad
to be hard at it: finally fabrics,
colours, candelabra,
the works!

How could the runners-after the
crowds running ahead, how could any of them
have known they'd find them-
selves there? I.e., at the
hangman's side? No,
on it? One by
one in the exhausted
afterwards, fidgeting, miserable, at
home, each had to find him-
self immured with the
undeservedly dead, for good.

What's "good"?
Springtime? The cat just
brought me a chewed
fledgling, his love-token.
                              The afterward
is a forever never knowing how
the cords of who and what we are
entwined and twisted so. I am

implicit in a
levigating of the incon-
venient scree, grinding it down with
the promise di-
versely given all of us.

Giver, I know now, anyone's
survival is to be on
Your side. If it is
not too late, may the many
be there, not to be eased, but to learn how
losing is not
negation. Oh it *is* that, but
inside-out, under the
merciful down-side-up of,
for example, sky.

The most lethal
bloodiest killer – in
cold blood – was
glint-eyed, even when un-
threatened. A
murderous tyrant brought to book,
he shouted down his ac-
cusers.
      Glum, un-
rubicund, the big man had
pressed his thumb down on
now this eager-eyed sycophant, now some
stolid fellows at hand, the
victimizers. No purple throttled
face loomed up in the Head's
silken window-corner.

Afterwards, some
having been inescapably
under that thumb, and not
protected by troops'
uniformed solidarity, still
had to be seen to, just a few
additional interments, dumpings-down.
Professional soldiers may,
no must, go off and
kill as ordered. Years

later the pictures rear and
scald.
        It had been not
so in the doing, in the on-
rush of another day, a
new hard-
driven dulling down.

A henchman's operatives, though,
rarely shrivel from the after-
math of having ·
produced those body-clumps. Untroubled
they seem, that they, for
secrecy's sake, may have to
be permanently suppressed.

Song from Swans

A swanherd stoops
out of his door too
early, too shivery. Preoccupied, he
brushes through the
rivery approaches. Grasses are
briefly festooned: dewdrops loll on
the tips till shone
on. They will
lift their tiny ·
granular green uncapped

tops to see and
be seen, 'way down below
eye level.

The swans this hour
are sleepy, honking a
little. But they are
singers. Their far
song, once in a
poem read about, he,
gruffly gentle with
them, longs to
one day hear.

Meanwhile it is
enough when the
steam is off the
skywide bowl over
this earth, its hills,
its rivers running, its
creatures cared for; even over
human beings, in
familied swarms or the
loners, a few. Humans alone must
shudder into morning
clothes, wrap up for
warmth, unthinking but
somehow, at this hour, blessed.

It is here necessary to
relive an afternoon when

I was age five or so. It still
haunts me some
sleepless nights. Next door
new neighbours had moved in.
"They have a girl your age. You'll have
a little friend . . ." (Why do
adults who do not always get along with
contemporaries like to assume that
children will?)
After a nap one day, I was put
out to play, with a
juicy B.C. apple in
my fist. And sure enough the
mother next door put out her
daughter too. But in a
fresh frock, after her rest, and
socks and buckled shoes, to wear to
Sunday School, maybe.
Not even to a
Sunday School picnic! And
not to a fenced backyard.
Yes, I craftily got her to
climb over and pull
a young carrot from our
vegetable patch while I
finished my apple – knowing the
hose had been on all morning.

If only she had let be!
Wasn't it *her* fault? She screwed up
her little pink face, all tears because of

muddied feet and smudgy white
socks. Pretending
rescue, I fouled her frilly
skirt, somehow, as well,
holding her by the
puff sleeve. And was
glad
when she went sobbing home.
I knew I had been bad, nor
to this day can I remember whether
she ever appeared to play again, thereafter.

Would it have made my
badness *evil* to have
co-opted the ones I usually played with to
gang up on
her or any other
defenceless stranger in our street?
Fortunately, we had
strenuous games: two
born leaders
made up their teams, picking us in
turn, till everyone was
brought in, even the last
chosen.

Are there human menaces who, under a
steely blade, are split
like rhizomes? Every broken piece
breeds further gnarling
roots. A
single harrowing finger has
to wriggle under, loosen the
hawser between the chunks, and
ease them
out.

How horrible to help
only by further
bedraggling some in-
fested barley field. But
look: its silvery silk has been
all overshadowed by those
stubborn knotted spikes
of alien twitch-grass.

What military map can plot
steps so drastic? Can some cadre de-
liberately, individu-
ally unsettle
raiders as ram-
paging as the Black
Death was
once? ("Bring out
your dead," the carters called

along the morning streets every
new day.)

What! Just let
it happen?

Animals kill for their cubs,'
their kittens,' sakes, or to survive a
disastrous season. But
what makes a here-and-there few
become ferocious, singled-out
"rogues"? Are these born fra-
tricidal? Is some cull a
callous, or cruel, necessity of natural
ORDER?

Don't answer. Shut the door.
Stay home. Be
calm-for-table company for one
another. Yes, to-
gether, sit it out.

No. Think.
The feral, fence-defying
wild ones must be
corralled.
Round them up we
must, be-
cause their pounces con-
tinue painful out there.
(Was pain their own

birthright?)
In the days of patriotic paci-
fism, after that Great
"War to end all wars," the double-
dutch finale, a high spin
out of the turning
ropes, was
"Turn your back on the KAI-SER."
The sense of the foreign was
reliably plucked from
the air, sheer non-
sense, tinted for
solemnity.

Perhaps, if diplomats had
early listened to their
light-heartedly prophetic little ones
at play . . . ?

How would it help to hand
the reins, even for a minute, to
such blue-sky-happy ones,
when they would be already
off on a different tack!

Back in Court

"A court of comedy," the man
set down in the dock

45

declared. His uninvited
defence was a new
threat: a hunger-strike!

He had commanded
force-feeding in his day
(also the water torture)
although he'd needed no
basis for finishing somebody
off.

These professional
lawyers would skirt
around pre-empting
anybody's right to toss his
life away.
Next day his rangy
brother drifted in among
other spectators in
night-wear, reportedly, or
so reporters told us.

On one court day the
prisoner veered
into an insolent disregard
of prosecutors or
their probings. Break
silence for these nobodies?
Not he.
"I'll slump awhile as though
half-asleep while those

trailing witnesses
moan away up there." But he
was too lively to
lie low for long!

No gnawings from
conscience? But perhaps a con-
science can be long
toothless, a jaw
hardened by chomping until
it's insensible.
                    Plea:
"I am
not responsible. I can-
not be held responsible"?

Soldiers and their
like (the other by
force co-opted ranks) quail
when the occurrences
must be suppressed for-
ever? They
shiver, shrug it off, for
now.

Some are beyond the pale? Con-
sidered EVIL, when they
rally susceptibles who must serve as
their
implements.

Let them
put on their robes, their
pathetic authority, up
there, on show to
jolt the massive chainmail of one who
only yesterday
declared: "I am
a Head of State."

"I WAS"? Was
that why he'd
shouted what had always been self-evident
before?

How *could* he see
himself as one
figure in a
column of figures
being added up to a
paltry "precedent"?

Nor did he know the
psalm's pronouncement: "the
God of Jacob . . . keeps
truth forever . . .
executes justice for
the oppressed."*

---

* "the God of Jacob . . . oppressed": from Psalm 146: 5–7.

Solution

Mischievous raccoons can gnaw through
cedar shingles! But
that is their way, a wry
swapping of natural and
proud constructed challenges to
such as he. In time the roof-
safe householders
take him
up on it. This
calls for something more than
caging overnight.

"Carry him off to
be released in
some far forest to forage
for better food than
city property-owners put
out in plastic or
metal cans with
lids the coons now
clatter under the midnight
windows." New
clamped-down lids appear to
frustrate the marauder
for
a day or two. Don't
put it past him to
figure it out.
Hear that? He's back, trying

to dent the can that
rolls away after the swivelling
lid. Who is in the lead?
animal? or man?

Relieved, one
falls back into a world of
roofed space, or away out
under the stars but in
darkness down among the
tall timbers.

AUGUST. READING

From lamplight on a glossy page
my eyes lift: now not
insects' footprints along
gleamy paper, but a
wash of diluted, cold
green tea with
dust-bunny clouds afloat
southward, grape-tinted once but
fast fading. A
last lick of
ivory light tinctures
a tall, very far over,
wall.

The lamplight gathers me
inside, with fabrics,
wood, some too-green apples, and a
blank screen, TV:
this is not
context. Spaces
close in here
but like a sky as if the
last, withdrawing, both
the one tenor: lucency.

        Here! All in
the same shivery
instant; every
tendril, thready root (or the ones
knuckled above ground),
creatures, feathered or
bald, or hugely hopeful towards
fur, or hairy; my
finger on this pen, too, each is
kept in being, in-
stant by instant.

Go high somewhere and
behold the trees'
naturally pastoring shadows, all
their subtly several greens.

Earfuls of almost
inaudible sighs,
rustling, tiny
needle-fall: why do we
thump and murmur in, so?
Because we're creatures in a
community, all
alive to imitative
delight.

Let stillness gather down at last,
then,
steeped in the oceanic
peacefulness of
greens, of leafiness,
of living and
listening.

SEASONAL SETBACKS

Does every Good have Enemies
and where, or are there Wardens?
Beetles chew in leafy trees
and aphids afflict gardens.

To walk in shade's all very well
when sun's honing its sickle;
But sticky threads a-dangle? Feel
your bare neck crawl and tickle!

Will next year's trees please have escaped
bowers in sorry tatters.
May every bough be simply draped
in the green that flatters.

Forested futures lie ahead:
aphids with no employer
go on relief and shrink instead
of serving the Destroyer.

SEVERN CREEK PARK

Awe is heartwhole. Those
multiplicitous trees are sky-
fingered at their
tips. Down in our
city's ravine, even by the
meandering footpath un-
scrolling in coolness, they
stand firm but sometimes
sigh. There are some
grassy flats too. There's a
cement bench warming itself.
When all is still
small constellations of gnats
glisten, wavering as
if in swollen light.

I, human, am heartsore from
stretching to
appropriate all that is
lavished here
until
it takes me in. I am
rinsed free of all but
eyes and
branch-bowered heart.

can winkle out
an unacknowledged
doubt, or a hedged memory
in the dim way of being
between His timelessnesses.

His nestlings are
sheltered within
deep-bosomed trees;
these raise soft domes, care
for the air. We breathe.
Underneath, when
stunned by sunmelt
their felt dimness is
shimmery rest.
Unquestioning at last,
much, lost or unremembered,
murmurs peacefully
under His
timeless largesse.

Glory, glory to the
eternal Who,
creator of
trees: the ones with
lanky dark green
leaves; delicate others of an
as-if-petalled leafiness, these
tip and dance
in the merest breath.

Yes, and the
green bay tree is a
cooling pavilion all
through a city July.
                    Why does
the Word miscast this
benison, the bay tree, as
"spreading evil"*? Save
that charge for
cannibalizing ivy, root and branch.
(Just see it wrench at
the crippling maiden elm,
out to deform it.)

---

* "spreading evil": Psalm 37:35 (King James Version)

Fingering sky, the linden
lifts. Its dappling
down here is no refuge; but
in the lovely youth of the year
its fragrance lingers, still
singing, afar.

Crabbed old oaks, your
season is autumn, late, on even into
first snow. Harbourer
of winds from the four
quarters of heaven: your
virtu.
      White
pine, blue spruce,
fir tree, yes, hemlock too:
the Who of their
kind can by
surprise, one
day, or evening, for
everyone, hush the heart.

There is a context to
breathing this forested city's
greenness: a bald
cumin-dark prairie
childhood, years of it, tirelessly
windy, bone-
drying, week upon week.

The surround signifies
when one has
one life only, be it
Toronto or Ant-
arctica, or the
Sea of Marmara, Who
knows.

JUST AFTER THE FALL EQUINOX

A galoshes morning
in No-
vember? Oh

        yes! And raddled
        sloshers out in the
        walkways shrug to
        minimalize
        tricklings down the neck.

Skyline at dawn was
hempen-tan. By now it's
dove-grey down into the
valley treetops, higher above
smudged, as evenly as though
an old pencil eraser
had been rubbed over and
over it
all.

        This is a day to welcome by
        wallowing through it. There's
        warmth in the magma we all
        float on; and some
        improbable candle reveals an
        implausible flickering
        hearth away inside for
        good – our mortal earth

mimicking one
magnified
planet,
ours!

Fishes my eyes meet
seldom. Possibly that time
was in a
dream.

Little furry people among
large tree roots, nibbling,
from their "hands," upright and
bright-eyed, remain
friends afar.

This, though,
truly happened, in the
heart of metropolitan Toronto.
The birds seem few now.
                                    Once
on Washington Avenue, a pale
first light touched the thin branches of
the pear tree in
its small backyard.
It might as well have been
a bank of footlights, for it
launched, instantly, a
whirl of little ones. They
twittered and piped and gurgled all
at once, each with its
colourful cravat or patch or
crest. They were all

breakfasting,
on their way south.

How still I sat! How a word formed
itself in air so gentled:
zephyr (stone-blue but soft).

Bird books give them
beautiful names, and
some peculiar ones.
Were they
calling to one another, or
to themselves, that morning?
They warble and
chirp, in memory now,
again, breaking but never
shattering every first-
light's quietude.

SAFE BUT SHAKY

I know I'm safe, but scared
for fear my fingers slip
or shakiness and dread
might make me lose my grip.

I play the misanthrope
in my own pantomime.
All's well, if I will cope
a minute at a time.

The Lord, who overheard
our thoughts, and understood
how all ways disappeared
when viewed too far ahead,

decided to provide
a (print) topography,
clues to the likely road
for us to choose if we

resolve to stay the course.
Doggedly pressing on,
it may go hard, or worse,
tangle in second-guessing.

Did You too face what seemed
options? We try to practise

steadiness. Round the bend
stray dazzles still distract us.

How do You guide us back?
In any case, we're sure
You've yielded us the slack
till, jerked, we know You're there.

Is Yours that western sky
aglow? Here shadows narrow
tonight along the way.
We'll rest now, till tomorrow.

HAG-RIDDEN

A plague of locusts is
a reminder that the
focus on knees and thighs
in stringy and gangling
insects can inspire in-
vidious
comparisons.
Nimble in
chain-armour (below) with an
upside-down carapace (shellacked),
these tiny
obstreperousnesses model
adoptable fashion trends.

The elderly, too,
are scant in under-
pinnings, and
angular. But,
unlike the locusts, these
swarm very seldom. Each may
go with a stick; a plague, perhaps first to
themselves. Yet, their
undemanding pleasure in the
world out under such a
mysterious (some days dazzling) sky
may be a to-be-
desired infection.

MORAL TALE, KITCHEN VARIETY

The pot who called the kettle black
ignored the risk of *quid pro quo:*
so when convivial chatter lagged
in came the tea-tray but NO TEA.

When kettle turned the tables, many
preferred the summer salad plate
though steaming bowls of stew were ready.
Still their last choice was – lemonade!

When pot and kettle both can pull
their weight, at need – and none, or few,
are ever indispensable –
then selfless service may ensue.
The fire that blackened pot *would* blacken kettle too!

OCCASIONAL POEM

You have to be a
teenager to brood
(*I* was when I wrote
a threnody about
an apple core)
on death, and somehow it
stirs you, then. For
the end of gleaming daylight, after
shut-eye darkness, isn't
suffocating when you are
indulging the black thrill of
"What if?"

To us who are
old the slippery slope
we're on seems a
benign
prospect although,
as realistic John
Bunyan noted, there's a
floundering in
that river. A
sunset glow is little
help to the frantic
struggler through a
worse-than-water,
swirling, element
first.

Someone suddenly
smitten though in
mid-career with
all flags flying for
good work accomplished and
challenges ahead,
gone? Yes.
Far out of any range
we can comprehend:
that, that, is *dead*'s
worst thud.

Art, and old
age, and (clearly, in
March) Toronto trees, are
each peculiar
root-systems, grappling
the heavens to earth to
make it secure. More-
over, each in its own
fashion fingers down
deep underground, in-
stinctively sure that nurture is
hidden there in the dark.
Treasure is what past living must have *become.*

The balanced branching-out is out
of sight? But art has
eyes there too. Old age,
nodding off, utters forth suddenly
words heard from an un-
known friend in the al-
ready dwindling dream.

                      Toronto
trees find rooted toes exploring far in
rainsoaked soil for ample
anchorage. How else
loosen those blowing
curtains of shadow summerseasons?

Then seeds may be
made for passing birds. Vertically
runnels are opened, pathways for insects'
feet. Some waver up the
leeside of the massive trunk.

Art has antennae always
in peril of pouncers, yet in-
domitably threading off into a
passing breeze. Art finds us
burrowing through our days, so
unroofs all usual places for
moments, irreversibly.
Old age excels
in listening. Voices sound
down the long corridors. This
opens beyond an unforeseen
gateway. To lift its
magic latch takes quiet
breathing. Curiosity is
unexacting, but expects
no less.

Toronto trees display the full
gamut of greens. These,
not the trees, age
in gold.

COMMUNAL CARE

The last leaves, linen-
pale but
large, stir on a
sapling's upper
tremulous limb.
Bare brambly shrubbery
protects them from
stinging November gusts.

Solstice will come, new
sunlight to
finger sapling and shrub,
invigorate observer and
observed. Each is absorbed
in this moving but usual
processional of *being*.

CLOUDS, FIVE P.M.

In late twilight snowclouds are
heaping up, above
a colourless backdrop. But
the last light pries a few
rifts, in eggy al-
bumin, astonishingly
here and there, *whipped* eggwhite
dabbed down as if with
a child's impetuous
impulse to put
finishing touches,
little curled peaks,
at random.

       Let the
gathering darkness draw
in now. December's first
flurry allows
flakes wide and high to
feel for freedom,
flying, wandering sideways,
falling upwards. Will early
morning's twilight show
hill and
dale distinct in white
outline?

Come to us, sky, and
grow; gather old earth in the
heaped-up garments you
wear, white, not
high; but
here!

SLOW BREATHING

What a quiet rainy interlude with
Christmas over, nothing
doing till New Year's – most
people still
recovering, or dutifully
dealing with the
fallout! (Even my
"list" isn't started yet. I mean
of presents, let alone cards.)
Guilt I have self-indulged me with too
long to learn that
guilt is an
ineffectual, transparent
veil
exposing rather than
excusing further
ducking of due
demands. Oh dear, like the
new year's, they're all
ahead up there!

Relax! The quiet light
falls on the undemanding pages of
a perhaps new
book, or an old
paper – not on
a proper yearly-presents' record,

(though such for yesteryears existed), no
nor any small-size
stationery. N.
                        B: allow no pen in hand
                unless a pushy
                poem blocks all al-
                ternatives even on
                December twenty-nine. The dishes
                are in the sink. It's past
                time for peeling carrots, pulling
                leftovers out of the fridge, putting the
                kettle on.

                Old age too is an
                unfestive interlude,
                lamplit, yes,
                but out of touch with all but
                a few, if any,
                kinfolk or old friends. Take
                heart! The seasonal
                sidewalks are lively still; once
                again ice-rinks resonate
                with bright dazzle, cornering blades, and thuds.
                                Remember that
                the longest stretches were the busy
                but beset ones, still remembered: offices,
                schedules. Losses.
                                These shatter
                the heart, ripen a
                person's experience before

the last-of-light is, once-
for-all, the new
threshold.

A SEQUEL

Ah, would that the writer's
life paralleled
a weed's life cycle!

In cities common young
grass
smiles sunward when
dandelions appear, small
suns themselves. Don't
gather them too soon: all you will have
is acrid staining mush.

In middle life their
faces become more
birds' heads, feathered in white, no
longer brash, a more heart-
fingering little old friend.

The white is to
remember when
the wind seeds dandelion progeny,
skyed, somewhere.

Back in the crunchy grass
the dandelion stems
wine-making ingatherers make
not least significant.

NOTES AND ACKNOWLEDGEMENTS

When Margaret Avison died in 2007, she left the almost-completed manuscript of *Listening*. A few clearly unfinished poems have not been included. "Our ? Kind," once considered as a title poem, mattered tremendously to Margaret. It was very close to being finished to her satisfaction. According to a note on a piece of scrap paper, she hoped to "anchor [this poem] in the free flow and delicate touch and effective/creative power of Goodness, in creation's beginning . . . and ending????" To this poem and others, a few changes (of the sort that experience tells us she would have accepted) have silently been made. *Listening* was prepared for publication by Stan Dragland and Joan Eichner.

"Occasional Poem" was written when Margaret's niece, Margaret McKim Ferguson, died in January 2006.

Bible quotations are from the New King James Version unless otherwise noted.

*

"Still Life" and "Metamorphosis" were published in *The New Quarterly* 95 (Summer 2005).

"Two Whoms *or* I'm in Two Minds" and "The Eternal One" were published in *Brick: A Literary Journal* (Summer 2008).

"Hag-ɽ ͻ ˋ" was published in PRISM *international* (Fall 200˥   ᴿest of Canadian Poetry in English, 2008 (Tig.   2008).